Inside every heart shines a
beautiful star –
words by Pietr
artwork: Marie Muravski

# A book by Pietr

## words to live by

shakeatambourine@gmail.com

# Inside every heart shines a beautiful star - some notes

Why I wrote this small book

well, for all of us, the world is full of complexities and trials.
That is not to say, it isn't also beautiful and mysterious. In
the midst of it all, there are certain helpful forces.
I wrote this as an encouragement to whoever reads it, also
to myself. It seems in every dark situation in the world,
there is a hidden light. In each difficulty, a pathway out, a
hope.
In every dark sky, a shining star. In fact, as you surely know,
we need the dark sky to see the stars. We can't see them in

the daylight.

## How this little book came about

There are not many words for this piece, but I've been carrying them around for many years, waiting for the right person to illustrate them. The first title I used was, "And then one day, you may find millions of sunflowers growing inside your heart," quite a long title.
At the time, the 90's, I was going through a lot of challenges and was writing a lot of spiritual words and manuscripts, many of which I still have.
This piece, was one of them.

## More on the imagery

There aren't a lot of words, as said, but they are concepts that I believe are in common with most faiths and forms of spirituality. There's a river, some stars, a planting field,  flowers, a farmer. There's consequences for both negative and positive actions. There's a stream that gathers itself together and flows past an obstacle. We are told, we can do the same. That is, to compose ourselves and gather strength. There are also stars, that shine above us and inside us. It's not religion, These are words aimed at clarity and hope.

## About me - Pietr

I've always loved writing, including songs, kids books, stories, poetry. My main interest is music and songwriting. I've had songs recorded by grammy artists and have also written a musical.

The artist Marie Muravski

As said I waited a long time to have the right artwork for these words. I was lucky to meet Russian artist, Marie Muravski. For me, she really nailed interpreting the images implicit in the words. She's a very gifted artist and got precisely the right feel for the little project, in my humble opinion.

My hopes

I write this to try and spread some positive vibes on the planet. There seems to be so much anger and fear in the world I see - I feel we all have so much in common, rather than differences. We are also an integral part of the web of nature and the natural processes of life. Decay, rebirth, flow are within and around us all the time. The images and words in this little book, *"Inside every heart shines a beautiful star,"* attempts to illustrate these processes, recognise them and try to work with them. This is what the tribal people's of the earth do and did so many years ago. Value nature and her lessons. I should mention, I was also impressed with Bruce Lipton's book, the 'Biology of belief,' as he spoke about the power of cooperation, rather than competition, as a model that moves us forward. He gives some compelling examples from the natural world. Let's hope this little book contributes a little bit to that cause..

Best

*Pietr*

# The bird

Inside every heart is a bird

that longs to fly

Longs to stretch out her wings
and soar above

the canyons of care

It doesn't matter
who you are,
where you live,
what you've done
or what you own,
this bird lives in your heart

Do not forget her,
she holds
your peace of mind
in her beak

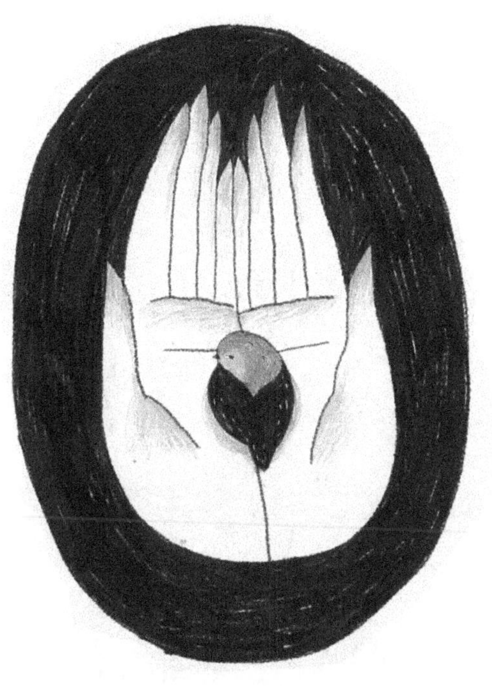

She is the same bird

Noah released from the ark

She is still
searching for you

# The Farmer

Every person
is also a farmer
that tends the fields of life.
Some grow weeds,
others, sunflowers

We know these things
by their fruits

Some tend their field
with love
and others with hate

Why is the latter surprised
when their fruit tastes bitter

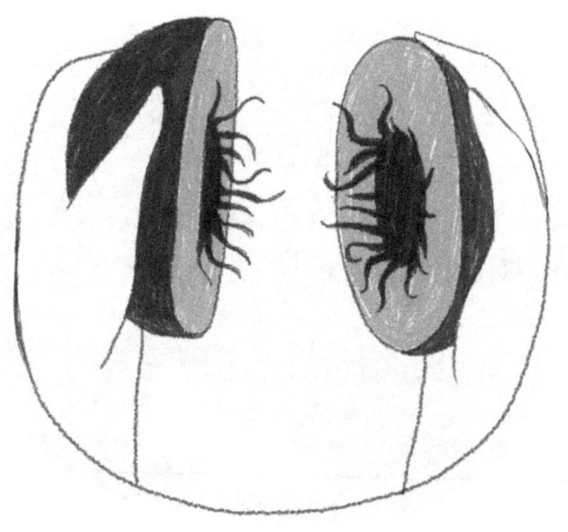

It is better
to plant the seeds of faith
in the meadows of your heart,

water them with care..

and shine on them
with your belief

and then one day
you may find millions
of sunflowers
growing in your heart

# The brook

Every person
is like a small brook,
flowing down a mountain
to the sea

The heart of this brook is clear,
but sometimes
it's waters become muddy.

This mud is made up
of too many possessions
and muddy thoughts

Too much mud
may impede your progress.
Sometimes a large stone
or a tree
may seem to stop the brook,

but it's waters just gather
into a large pool
and then
flow past the obstacle.

You can do the same!

# The Tree

Every person is also a leaf
on the tree of life.
They may not see
the roots of this tree,
but they are what nourishes
every leaf on the tree

They may not realise
that every leaf on this tree
is their brother and sister,
but this is true

They may not realise
that they are part
of a great cycle
that includes the earth,
the sun
and the rain,
but this is also true

they may not realise
that when they fall
they will become a part of the earth,
from which all life will grow

So, if you have had losses
in your life
consider them to be
like fallen leaves,
from which new life
will surely grow

# The Star

Lastly,
inside every heart,
shines a beautiful star

The darker the sky,
the brighter the star

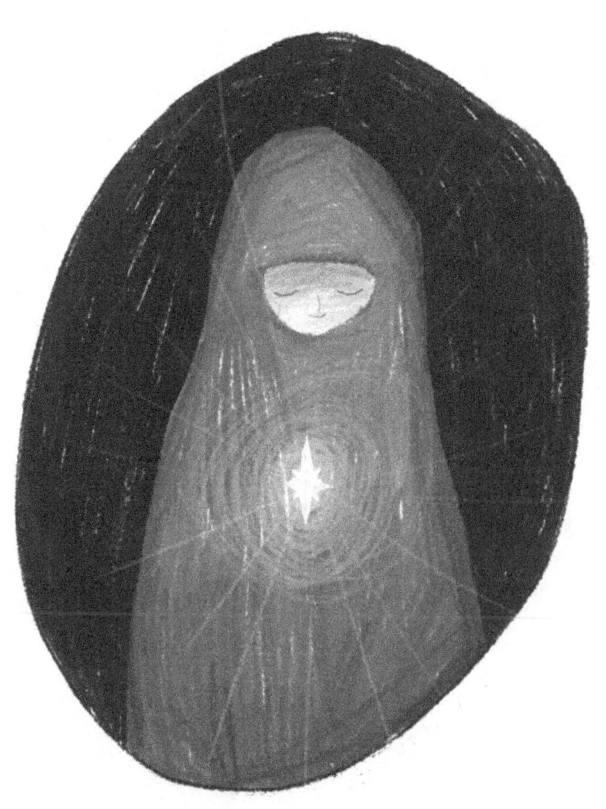

If you are a sailor
who is lost,
you can chart your course
by this special star

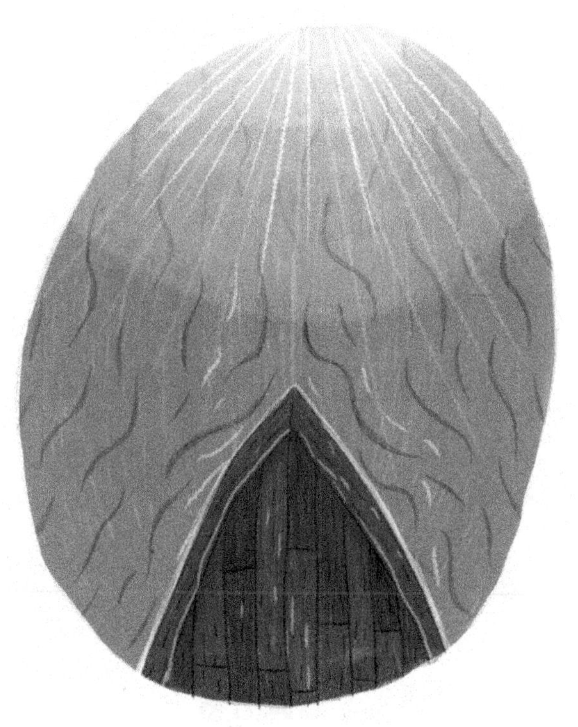

Even when the waters
of the sea rage
and strong winds
veer you from your path,
this star is there for you

Even if clouds obscure it,
it is still there

So if you have troubles,
look up in the sky
of your heart
and you will see
this beautiful star
shining - just for you!

Another book by Pietr
*Heavens above*
with words by Pietr and beautiful sketches
by Marie Muravski. If you're interested in
ordering this, please write to:
shakeatambourine@gmail.com